Tech 2.0

World-Changing Social Media Companies

Twitter

by Craig Ellenport

Tech 2.0

World-Changing Social Media Companies

Facebook®

Instagram®

Reddit®

Snapchat®

Twitter®

WhatsApp®

Tech 2.0

World-Changing
Social Media
Companies

Twitter®

by Craig Ellenport

Mason Crest

Mason Crest
450 Parkway Drive, Suite D
Broomall, PA 19008
www.masoncrest.com

Series ISBN: 978-1-4222-4060-1
Hardback ISBN: 978-1-4222-4065-6
EBook ISBN: 978-1-4222-7732-4

First printing
1 3 5 7 9 8 6 4 2

Produced by Shoreline Publishing Group LLC
Santa Barbara, California
Editorial Director: James Buckley Jr.
Designer: Patty Kelley
www.shorelinepublishing.com
Cover photographs by Worawee Mepian/Dreamstime.com

Library of Congress Cataloging-in-Publication Data
Names: Ellenport, Craig, author. Title: Twitter / by Craig Ellenport.
Description: Broomall, PA : Mason Crest, [2018] | Series: Tech 2.0: world-changing social media companies | Includes index.
Identifiers: LCCN 2017058189| ISBN 9781422240656 (hardback) | ISBN 9781422240601 (series) | ISBN 9781422277324 (ebook)
Subjects: LCSH: Twitter (Firm)--Juvenile literature. | Twitter--Juvenile literature. | Online social networks--Juvenile literature.
Classification: LCC HM743.T95 E45 2018 | DDC 302.30285--dc23 LC record available at https://lccn.loc.gov/2017058189

QR Codes disclaimer:

CONTENTS

Introduction: **What's in a Tweet?** 6

Chapter 1: Hatching Twitter 10

Chapter 2: Global Dominance 24

Chapter 3: The Evolving World of Twitter . . 36

Chapter 4: The Consciousness of the World . 50

Find Out More 62

Series Glossary of Key Terms 63

Index 64

KEY ICONS TO LOOK FOR

Words to Understand: These words with their easy-to-understand definitions will increase the reader's understanding of the text, while building vocabulary skills.

Sidebars: This boxed material within the main text allows readers to build knowledge, gain insights, explore possibilities, and broaden their perspectives by weaving together additional information to provide realistic and holistic perspectives.

Educational Videos: Readers can view videos by scanning our QR codes, providing them with additional educational content to supplement the text. Examples include news coverage, moments in history, speeches, iconic moments, and much more!

Text-Dependent Questions: These questions send the reader back to the text for more careful attention to the evidence presented here.

Research Projects: Readers are pointed toward areas of further inquiry connected to each chapter. Suggestions are provided for projects that encourage deeper research and analysis.

Series Glossary of Key Terms: This back-of-the-book glossary contains terminology used throughout this series. Words found here increase the reader's ability to read and comprehend higher-level books and articles in this field.

Introduction
What's in a Tweet?

I n 2011, the editors of the Merriam-Webster Collegiate Dictionary added a new definition of the word "tweet." Since the year 1768, the dictionary had defined tweet as simply "a chirping note." As of 2011, a second definition of the word was "a post made on the Twitter online message service."

Oh, but it is so much more than that.

A tweet can be a statement, an opinion, an announcement. It might be a question that results in more tweets from people who think they have the answer. It can be breaking news, reaction to breaking news, public service announcements, safety alerts. It can be a photo or a video. It can be a live video stream of a sporting event or a concert. It can be an advertisement or a campaign designed to build awareness for a brand. It can be messages from a celebrity to his or her fans. It can be updates from a professional sports team.

It can be a proclamation from the president of the United States.

Whatever the message, tweets are delivered through Twitter, the social media platform that was created in 2006 and has since become a ubiquitous presence in modern society.

How ubiquitous? This is how Twitter defines itself in official company press releases:

"Twitter, Inc., is what's happening in the world and what people are talking

Why 140?

To provide you with the ultimate example of how much a user can express in a tweet, this is a sentence that contains exactly 140 characters.

So how did the folks who created Twitter settle on the original 140 characters?

Well, the foundation for Twitter was based in SMS—text messaging from cell phones. At the time, text messaging was limited to 160 characters. So the Twitter braintrust decided that tweets would be no longer than 140 characters—which would allow up to 20 characters for the username that appears before the tweet.

One of the advantages of Twitter was that users could send and receive tweets through their phones—but they were delivered as text messages, and thus users were charged a fee for texting. If a tweet were more than 160 characters, it would be sent as multiple texts, so it would cost twice as much. This was long before the days where unlimited text messaging was common, so it was an important consideration.

Over the years, Twitter users have come up with clever abbreviations to fit their messages within 140 characters. Of course, they've also taken to expressing thoughts in a series of related tweets, something that has come to be known as a "tweetstorm." As explained on page 40, Twitter made the move to expand the limit to 280 in 2017.

about right now. On Twitter, live comes to life as conversations unfold, showing you all sides of the story. From breaking news and entertainment to sports, politics and everyday interests, when things happen in the world, they happen first on Twitter."

Sounds impressive, and the numbers back it up. According to Omnicore, a digital marketing agency, here are some staggering statistics regarding usage of Twitter, and the numbers continue to grow:

- 330 million monthly active Twitter users
- 500 million tweets sent per day
- 100 million daily active users

Here's a number that might be the most staggering, and certainly the most important to the more than 3,000 employees of the company: The business world says the value of Twitter, Inc., exceeds $25 billion.

Twitter is unique among the major social media networks in that it truly brings together "social"—everyday people sharing thoughts and experiences—with "media"—news organizations and their reporters telling us what is happening in the world in real time.

As of late 2017, Twitter.com was among the top 15 most popular websites on the internet overall and second only behind Facebook among social media networks.

1

Hatching Twitter

S trange as it may sound, the origins of Twitter can be traced back to a young teenager listening to a police scanner. That young teenager was Jack Dorsey (left), who would become one of the co-creators of Twitter as well as other groundbreaking technological advancements.

Growing up in St. Louis, Missouri, Dorsey was the son of an engineer. His father's job gave Dorsey access to computers before most of the other kids his age. He first began playing with computers at the age of eight. That was in 1984, and most adults didn't even have computers back then.

But merely using computers was not enough for Dorsey; he wanted to understand how they worked. He taught himself how to build computer programs at a time when his fellow students didn't even know how to use a computer. All this took place before he was even a teenager.

Dorsey's other passion was trains, and it went hand-in-hand with his interest in technology. He decorated his room with posters of maps and trains,

WORDS TO UNDERSTAND

functionality the ability of a product to be successfully used

urban planner a person who puts together designs and plans for cities, including buildings, open space, utilities, and transportation all the while thinking about how the city was connected in one large grid. Dorsey has said that if he hadn't become so interested in computers, he might have become an **urban planner** instead. He wanted to get to the heart of how vehicles moved and communicated. He used a police scanner to pick up radio signals transmitted from emergency vehicles moving through his area of town. The way the people in the vehicles communicated with one another fascinated Dorsey.

"They're always talking about where they're going, what they're doing, and where they currently are," he said.

Dorsey used a police scanner like this one that later inspired Twitter.

The people he listened to on the police scanner did not speak in full sentences. Instead, they used short codes to communicate what was happening. Dorsey thought this was very efficient, and began thinking of ways these short bursts of communication could be used in other areas of life. The signals he listened to through his police scanner became his very first inspiration for the future creation of Twitter.

An Idea Forms

While still in college, Dorsey was already a programming wizard in great demand. He dropped out of New York University and began to think about how technology could be used to improve the world. He reflected on the dispatch conversations he listened to as a child and thought of ways to apply that thinking to the internet, which was now expanding rapidly. When he began working for a podcasting company in 2005, his dreams began to take shape.

Dorsey saw a clear connection between the internet and the increasing use of cell phones. "Now, we all have these cell phones. We had text messaging. Suddenly we could update where I was, what I'm doing, where I'm going, how I feel. And then it would go out to the entire world," he said in an interview.

At the time, smartphones were uncommon and just starting to come out. If Jack wanted to connect everyday people to the internet through cell phones, he would need to do it through text messages. Dorsey wasted no time pitching his new idea to his new employer, Odeo. One former executive recounted the experience: "He came to us with this idea: 'What if you could share your status with all your friends really easily, so they know what you're doing?'" Odeo was interested in his idea for Twitter, which he referred to as "twttr" when the project first began. The short name, which is credited to Odeo colleague Noah Glass, came from the trend at the time to keep abbreviations short. When users received a text from Twitter, it would be distributed from the abbreviation twttr, and the SMS code 40404. Developers of the website hoped the code would be easy for users to memorize and recognize.

Jack received help for his new project from Biz Stone, Odeo's creative director, and another contractor named Florian Weber. All three were very talented programmers, and they were able to build the first version of Twitter within two weeks.

On March 21, 2006, Jack sent out his first Twitter update (an update wasn't called a "tweet" until 2007). It said, "just setting up my twttr." Only Odeo employees used the first version of Twitter, as it was not ready to be shared with the world.

The developers of Twitter spent a lot of money testing the **functionality** of the website. Having an unlimited text-message plan was almost unheard of at the time, so they were forced to pay for each individual text message that was sent or received during testing. They racked up thousands of dollars in SMS charges to

Biz Stone was one of the first people Dorsey brought in to help build Twitter.

their phones during this time.

Fortunately, this investment would eventually prove it was all worth it. Everything began to change starting in July 2006 when Twitter was released publicly. It took off very slowly at first, but showed a lot of promise.

Jack Dorsey, Biz Stone, and Evan Williams created a new company, which they named Obvious Corporation. They also acquired Odeo and every asset Odeo owned. One year later, Twitter branched off as its own company.

Gaining Users

Jack and his team were finding it hard to get people to use Twitter, and the reasons were obvious. Evan Williams explained why in a 2013 interview: "With Twitter, it wasn't clear what it was," he began. "They called it a social network, they called it micro-blogging, but it was hard to define, because it didn't replace anything. There was this path of discovery with something like that, where over time you figure out what it is."

Williams was correct; Jack and his team needed to figure

The annual tech conference called SXSW saw a Twitter breakout.

out exactly how users would see Twitter before they began advertising it.

That moment came in 2007, at the South by Southwest Interactive Conference in Austin, Texas. This large conference features emerging technology that has not yet gained popularity in the world. It is known to foster great ideas for the future.

Twitter was right at home at the South by Southwest Interactive Conference. Dorsey and his team set up computer monitors where attendees could see the tweets of other users. The service was mentioned by panelists and speakers, which greatly increased the number of people who used Twitter during the conference. Tweets tripled from 20,000 per day to 60,000 per day while the conference took place. At the end of the conference, Twitter received a Web Award.

Many of Twitter's first users were everyday people talking about their lives, but the service caught on quickly. It didn't take more than a year before celebrities and other famous people began using the service for their own needs. Both 2008 presidential candidates, Barack Obama and John McCain, used Twitter to keep in touch with their supporters while campaigning.

The Many Uses of Twitter

Expanding websites are prone to outages, or periods of time where the website is simply overloaded with users and cannot function properly, causing the website to crash. Twitter's rapid growth from 2007 to 2008 led to many of these outages, and the service has experienced periodic outages ever since. Fortunately, these outages only occur a few times a year, and they are usually due to an unusual spike in activity. Regular maintenance is performed to expand Twitter's servers as the website continues to grow.

In 2009, a market-research company did a study to figure out exactly how people were using Twitter. The research found that 40 percent of tweets were about "pointless babble." Another 38 percent were conversational tweets between users. Only 4 percent of posts were about news, with another 4 percent being taken up by spam posts. Six percent of posts involved self-promotion, while nine percent of tweets were retweeted to pass along information.

Soccer's Cristiano Ronaldo has a huge following.

Birth of the Hashtag

Twitter users have greatly defined how Twitter is used, but they have also inspired new functionality within the website. For example, users began using hashtags long before they were officially supported by Twitter. Hashtags were invented as a way to communicate ideas within text. They are created by typing a pound symbol followed by any combination of words. One example of a hashtag would be #hashtag.

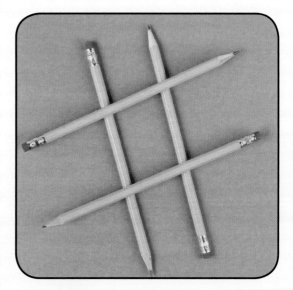

These hashtags were used to explain what a post was about in as few characters as possible. After all, users only had 140 characters to work with! A user posting about politics might put #politics at the end of a post. At first, these hashtags were only text markings and could not be interacted with in any other way. This all changed in July of 2009 when hashtags were officially adopted by Twitter.

From that point forward, any hashtag became a link that users could click to view any other posts that contained the same hashtag. It was an easy way to search for people who were talking about the same thing, and it made the Twitter community feel more connected than ever before. So if you are new to Twitter and don't have many followers, that's okay. If you add #politics to a post, anyone who searches that hashtag can see your post.

One of the ways people use Twitter is to discuss current events. This is a great way to pass on information long before others can catch it on the news or any other social media website. The servers that host Twitter undergo more strain during a very popular event, such as a large sports game or media award show. These events can temporarily shut the servers down for minutes or even hours.

As Twitter grew on an international level, people were using the service to share their experiences with users from around the world. In 2009, many Iranian people were using Twitter to communicate with each other about ongoing protests in the country.

Twitter's political impact

Protests like this one in Washington DC helped inspire Twitter to assist Iranians.

Twitter had planned to have a scheduled maintenance during this time, but a US State Department spokesperson asked Twitter to delay the maintenance so that people in Iran could communicate—and Twitter agreed!

Thanks to Twitter, the whole world is now linked together in one large network. All users have to do is type a short 140- to 280-character tweet.

Although Twitter has many possible uses, most users treat it as a micro-blogging service. In other words, they post small snippets about their day on Twitter for their followers to see. They might talk about how they are feeling about an upcoming test, what they are eating at the moment, or what movie they plan to see later on tonight. This is exactly how Dorsey envisioned the average person would use Twitter when he created it in the first place.

"Now I can see the entire world, and how they're thinking, and how they're feeling, and what they're doing, and what they

Dorsey was the public face of Twitter in its early, startup days.

care about, and where they're going," Dorsey said in an interview. Twitter became exactly what he hoped it would be.

Dorsey was once asked about his proudest moment regarding the invention of Twitter. He said, "I am most proud of how quickly people came to it and used it in a million different ways." People are finding different ways to use Twitter each day.

Text-Dependent Questions

1. How were Twitter messages first received?

2. Who was the main creator of Twitter?

3. What country did Twitter help with communications in 2009?

Research Project

The inventors of Twitter were breaking new ground in how people communicate. Look at the ways you and your friends connect . . . what would you do differently if you could? What services or programs do you think should be created? How would they work? Make a list (you might discover your own Twitter!).

2

Global Dominance

n April 2007, just one month after Twitter made its first big splash at the South by Southwest Conference, the decision was made to have Twitter "spin off" from Odeo and become its own company. After all, Odeo was a podcasting company. Twitter was just an idea created by some Odeo employees—it had nothing to do with podcasting. Besides, Odeo was not doing very well as a business. Twitter, on the other hand, had great potential.

Soon after forming its own company, Twitter announced its first round of funding from **venture capitalists**. This was money being invested in the company by big financial groups that were betting on the future success of Twitter. The company raised $5 million through this first round of funding, and it was valued at $20 million. A year later, Twitter secured another round of funding. One of the new investors in Twitter was Jeff Bezos, the founder of Amazon.

Twitter was becoming a major player in Silicon Valley, the area in Northern California where many of the newest digital technology companies were making a name for themselves. Still, even as more and more people were signing up and using Twitter, it was hard to explain exactly what it was.

"Twitter is a way to keep connected to your friends," Dorsey explained

WORDS TO UNDERSTAND

revenue money that a company brings in from its products or services

venture capitalists people who invest money in young companies in hopes they will grow greatly in value

in an interview. "It's basically mini-blogging." Because tweets—originally known as "updates"—were limited to 140 characters, these updates were short and focused. "They're usually personal, and they're about just random things you're doing during the day instead of being a very composed article," said Dorsey.

In that same interview, Twitter co-founder Evan Williams said another way to think of Twitter is "present-tense blogging." Most blogs, he explained, talked about things that happened in

The 2009 Hudson River plane crash proved the use of Twitter.

the past, maybe yesterday. Twitter, on the other hand, was more about what's happening right now.

A perfect example of this was what happened on January 15, 2009. That's the day US Airways Flight 1549 left LaGuardia Airport and almost immediately lost all engine power after striking a flock of geese. The plane's pilot, Chesley "Sully" Sullenberger, became a national hero when he successfully made an emergency landing on the Hudson River. One of the first images of the plane floating off the coast of Manhattan was posted on Twitter by Janis Krums, who was on a ferry that just happened to be in the vicinity. As Krums tweeted along with the photo, the ferry he was on proceeded to pick up passengers from the plane.

This was one of countless examples of how Twitter became more than just a social network for people to keep in touch with friends. It helped coin the term "citizen journalist"—giving anyone with a Twitter account the ability to document news they happened to witness.

The Media and Celebrities Jump In

Of course, established media outlets also started to recognize the value of Twitter as a way to drive traffic to their websites and TV channels. In 2009, CNN—Cable News Network—had one of the most popular Twitter accounts. Their handle, @CNNBreakingNews, was seen as a valuable Twitter account for followers who wanted to stay updated on the latest news and

Tweets From Space

By 2010, Twitter was a global phenomenon. The social networking platform had about 100 million active users all over the world.

While tweets were being sent from all corners of the planet, history was made on January 22, 2010, when astronaut T. J. Creamer sent the first tweet from outer space.

"Hello Twitterverse! We r now LIVE tweeting from the International Space Station - the 1st live tweet from Space! :) More soon, send your ?s"

This breakthrough had more to do with NASA than with Twitter. Previously, astronauts had been able to tweet indirectly from space by emailing their tweets back to Earth and having somebody else tweet for them. The space agency upgraded software to allow for personal access to the internet through wireless connection.

For NASA, this was much more than a publicity stunt, and it reinforced the importance of Twitter as a means for connecting people. Just as Twitter was seen as a valuable way for people around the world to be connected, NASA recognized that having the ability to tweet from space gave its astronauts who were in space for long periods of time a closer connection to their family and friends back home.

information. CNN Breaking News had nearly one million followers.

Actor Ashton Kutcher also had one of the most popular early accounts on Twitter, simply because he was a celebrity with interesting and funny things to say. Kutcher decided he wanted to challenge CNN Breaking News and become the first account on Twitter with one million followers. On April 16, 2009, he accomplished that mission.

Actor Ashton Kutcher was one of the early Twitter proponents.

"We now live in an age in media that a single voice can have as much power and relevance on the web, that is, as an entire media network," he said, appearing on the CNN show Larry King Live. "And I think that to me was shocking."

A day later, Kutcher and Twitter co-founder Biz Stone appeared on *The Oprah Winfrey Show*—at which time Oprah Winfrey posted the first tweet on her account. Winfrey already had 73,000 followers before her tweet. Later that day, she had more than 100,000 followers. As of 2017, Winfrey has tweeted more than 12,000 times, and had nearly 40 million followers.

"Twitter has experienced watershed events over the last two years since we founded the company, and momentum continues

Even the Dalai Lama himself has seen the value of a Twitter feed.

to build," Stone wrote in an email to CNN on the day of *Oprah* appearance. "Certainly having Oprah and Ashton embrace Twitter so enthusiastically will be another big moment for us."

Kutcher, however, was quick to point out that Twitter shouldn't be thought of just as a way for celebrities to spread their message. It was for anyone and everyone.

"I think it's really important that Twitter is not about celebrities," he told Larry King. "It's not a platform for celebrities . . . It's really about everyday people having a voice. And I don't want it to be dwarfed by celebrity."

Following in Kutcher's footsteps, many more celebrities—

like Justin Bieber and Katy Perry—became Twitter sensations. But so did news organizations and even world leaders. The Dalai Lama, who is the spiritual leader of the Tibetan Buddhists, joined Twitter in 2009 and currently has more than 15 million followers.

Politicians also quickly discovered the power of Twitter— the ability to spread their message to the masses. It cost a lot of money to run an ad on television, but sending out a tweet was free.

In 2007, then-Senator Barack Obama joined Twitter. A year later, Twitter proved to be a valuable tool in his successful campaign for president.

But the fact that high-profile Twitter users had such huge followings was a reminder that the majority of Twitter users were not famous people or big companies. The numbers were staggering.

In 2007, it was estimated that users posted an average of 5,000 tweets per day. In 2009, that number exploded to 35 million tweets a day.

The Business of Twitter

While Twitter had become an international phenomenon and one of the most popular of the new and emerging social media networks, there was still uncertainty as to how the business was going to succeed. If anybody could sign up for a Twitter account and use the service for free, how would Twitter make money?

With venture capitalists investing millions of dollars in Twitter, the need to solve that problem became more important than ever. There were several changes in the leadership of the company. First, Jack Dorsey stepped down as chief executive officer and was originally replaced by co-founder Evan Williams, who had more business experience than Dorsey. Eventually, Williams was replaced by a new CEO, Dick Costolo.

When Costolo started working for Twitter in 2009, the

Dick Costolo was brought in to provide Twitter with new leadership.

company had yet to earn a single penny in profit. They had plenty of money from investors, but there was no plan in place for the business to actually earn money.

Costolo immediately changed that. The first thing he did was strike deals with tech giants Google and Microsoft. While Twitter wasn't making money at that point, they did have was a huge amount of "user data." Twitter was getting more than 20 million unique visitors a month. It was extremely valuable for companies like Google and Microsoft to know what people were doing on Twitter—what products they were buying, what TV shows they were watching, where these people were from.

An inside look at Twitter

That was a good start, but Costolo also knew that the majority of Twitter's **revenue** was going to come from advertising. In April 2010, the company announced that it would begin to sell ads in the form of what it called "promoted tweets."

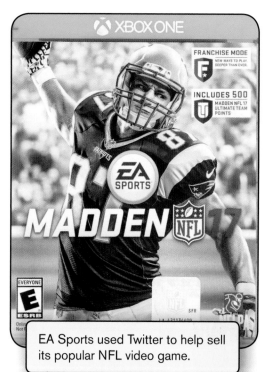

EA Sports used Twitter to help sell its popular NFL video game.

These weren't banner ads or pop-up ads that appear on most websites. Promoted tweets looked like other tweets appearing in users' timelines. More importantly, different users saw different promoted tweets, depending on their interests. In other words, if a user follows a lot of bands or music-related accounts, there's a good chance they might see an ad for the streaming-music service Spotify. If they follow a lot of football teams, they might see a promoted tweet for EA Sports' new NFL video game.

Costolo hired more than 400 new employees to become Twitter's ad sales team. Before long, the money started to come.

A big advantage of running ads as "promoted tweets" is that they don't look any different depending on where the user is seeing them. As more and more people around the world were accessing the internet through smartphones, many consumer websites were having a hard time figuring out how to best make advertisements presentable on a small screen. By 2015, it was reported that nearly 80 percent of all Twitter users accessed the service through mobile devices.

"Promoted Tweets fit naturally within the product, wherever it goes," said one Twitter executive in a 2015 story in *Wired* magazine. "Everybody else had a struggle when they switched to mobile. But we were already there."

Text-Dependent Questions

1. From whom did Twitter get most of its original investment?

2. Who took over from Dorsey as CEO?

3. How did Twitter finally figure out how to make money?

Research Project

Check out a Twitter feed, either your own or a friend's. See if you can figure out how each of the first 10 promoted tweets you see reached that feed. What factors do you think connected the ad and the user? How did Twitter connect your or your friend's interests with the company's or service's?

twitter

3

The Evolving World of Twitter

When Jack Dorsey and the small group of programmers at Odeo began working on Twitter in 2006, it took them two weeks to come up with an application that would essentially allow users to send the equivalent of text messages through the internet. The technology was a combination of how text messages were being delivered through cell phones and how "instant messages" were being sent online through services such as AOL Instant Messenger.

Over the years, as Twitter grew into a social networking behemoth, its programmers faced greater challenges, not least of which was how to keep the platform working smoothly despite the increased volume of activity. In its early years, Twitter dealt with numerous service **disruptions**. At first, these issues often occurred during events that were popular in the technology community, since they were the early adopters of Twitter. Eventually, users started seeing a disruption of service when major news stories were taking place, such as when pop star Michael Jackson died on June 25, 2009. Twitter recorded 50,000 tweets about Jackson in a one-hour span, causing the service to run

WORDS TO UNDERSTAND

brevity shortness, briefness

disruptions breaks in any otherwise steady program or process

open-source describing a computer program that can be used by any programmer to create or modify the product

very slowly in the hours that followed.

The good news for Twitter is that these problems were being caused because more and more people were using the service. That popularity led to more investment dollars, and the company wisely used that money to hire more engineers and programmers to not only fix the problems but also add more features to Twitter that would keep users engaged. In fact, of the 3,200 employees at Twitter in 2017, about 40 percent work in technology roles.

What's interesting about the new features that Twitter has rolled out over the years is that many of them were the brainchild of users. People using the service actually came up with the word "tweet." And because Twitter has always been an **open-source** product—meaning anyone can see the original source code and tinker with it—users have been able to lend a hand in improving it.

"A lot of our history is really around people using the service inventing ways of doing things on the service," said Dorsey. "The @username, the hashtag, the retweet. . . . It's really meaningful when you build a brand that people can bring their own personality and their own invention and product to, because that means you haven't just built a product. You've actually built a platform, and people can build upon that platform and make their own thing. And if they feel ownership over that, they'll continue using it in really interesting ways."

Talking Twitter

In addition to the hashtag, which has become such a common feature that it is a regular part of culture beyond Twitter, other add-on features that have helped Twitter grow include:

Direct Messages: Private messages sent from one Twitter account to one or more other accounts; one-on-one or group private conversations.

Retweets: Users can forward a tweet on their timeline so that all of their followers can see it.

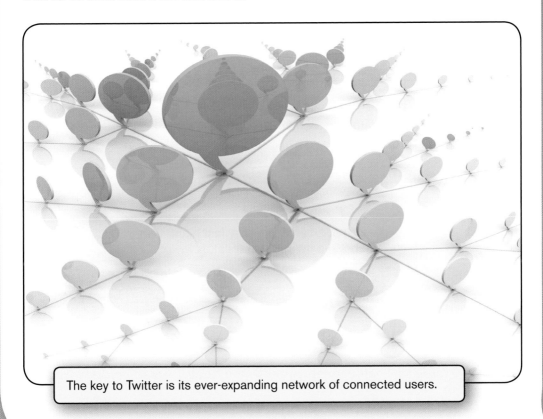

The key to Twitter is its ever-expanding network of connected users.

Tech 2.0

Longer Tweets

The concept of Twitter was born out of text messaging and 160 was the character limit for SMS messages, so Twitter followed suit. Allowing up to 20 characters for a username, the decision was made to limit updates to 140 characters. It's been that way ever since, and the 140-character limit has been a defining trait that sets Twitter apart from other social networks.

But that may be changing.

On September 26, 2017, Twitter announced it would be expanding to a limit of 280 characters in some languages, including English.

"When people don't have to cram their thoughts into 140 characters and actually have some to spare, we see more people Tweeting," the company wrote in a blog post.

Twitter had considered expanding the character count for years. There was even a time when they considered expanding the limit to 10,000 characters—which essentially would have changed Twitter

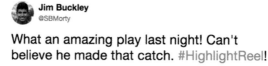

Jim Buckley
@SBMorty

What an amazing play last night! Can't believe he made that catch. #HighlightReel!

1:19 PM - 18 Aug 2017

♡ 1   ⇄   ♡   ᵢₗᵢ

Jim Buckley
@SBMorty

That was the greatest Super Bowl I've ever seen! It was like neither team wanted to play defense. I'm glad I've got more space than ever to write about that #SuperBowl on my Twitter feed!

4:39 PM - 6 Feb 2018

from a micro-blogging service to a full-out blogging service. That idea was rejected.

In recent years, Twitter had made other tweaks to make it easier for users to fit their tweets into 140 characters. It used to be that attaching a photo used up some characters, depending on the size of the photo, but that is no longer the case. Likewise, the inclusion of an @username no longer counts toward the character limit.

"This is a small change, but a big move for us," Twitter co-founder Jack Dorsey tweeted when the 280-character announcement was made. "140 was an arbitrary choice based on the 160-character SMS limit. Proud of how thoughtful the team has been in solving a real problem people have when trying to tweet. And at the same time maintaining our **brevity**, speed, and essence!"

Lists: Users can create lists, which are sub-groups of accounts they follow. So if you follow a wide variety of accounts, you can create a list that follows a specific group.

Trending Topics: Based on hashtag usage, you can see what other people are talking about on Twitter. You can search trending topics based on a specific location or all over the world.

URL shorteners: One of the toughest obstacles to keeping a tweet within the 140-character limit was the inclusion of a link that had a long URL. A few different companies offered this service, in which you enter a URL on their site and it gets converted into a shorter URL. Eventually, Twitter offered this service itself.

Need for Video

By the end of 2012, Twitter had more than 200 million monthly active users. As popular as it was, however, Twitter was far from the only game in town when it came to social media. Facebook had been around since 2004 and was the clear giant of the industry, but the platforms were different enough that they could easily coexist. However, newer social media platforms that could be seen as competition for Twitter were starting to emerge. The biggest competitors were Instagram and Snapchat, social networks that were growing rapidly thanks to a younger base that embraced the idea of sharing photos and videos.

On Twitter, it was easy to share a link to videos, but watching a video would require clicking the link and opening a web

The acquisition of Vine brought increased video presence to Twitter.

browser. Recognizing the need to incorporate video into its platform, Twitter bought a company called Vine, which launched in January 2013. Vine enabled users to post six-second videos. When shared on Twitter, Vine videos played directly in users' Twitter feeds.

Vine was an instant success. Like video-sharing giant YouTube, Vine saw some of its more creative users gain celebrity status. Some, like pop singer Shawn Mendes, were able to use their success on Vine to launch a music career. However, Vine as a company faced the same issue its parent company had: how does it make money?

Before Vine could figure that out, Twitter was already moving on in its quest to succeed with video. Executives at Twitter came to an important realization: Rather than compete with television for viewers, Twitter could partner with TV networks and other broadcasters to create the "second-screen experience." In other words, fans of HBO's *Game of Thrones* could watch the

Even the mighty NFL has seen the power of Twitter's huge audience.

Promoted tweets and how they work

show on Sunday night and tweet about it live using #GoT in their tweets to share with others who are watching.

In May 2013, the company launched Twitter Amplify, which gave media partners the ability to post real-time video clips. The National Football League was one of the first partners to sign up, and the deal made perfect sense. Twitter was able to post exclusive NFL highlight videos—valuable content for its users and also a strong promotional vehicle to encourage those users to watch more football on TV. What's more, Amplify videos included ads that ran before or after the content they were promoting. NFL sponsors such as McDonald's, Verizon, and Microsoft paid millions of dollars to have their ads included in the Amplify videos. This revenue was shared by the NFL and Twitter.

Within a year of launching Amplify, Twitter had signed up 70 media partners, including all four major broadcast networks. The sports and entertainment worlds found that Twitter provided an excellent companion for major live events such as the Academy Awards and the Super Bowl. Media partnerships became a growing business for Twitter. A sports partnership team was formed to meet with leagues and teams to help them create new ways to utilize their Twitter accounts.

Few partners are as aware of the role Twitter plays in keeping their fans engaged as the National Basketball Association.

Trump faced Clinton in a 2016 debate, also seen on Twitter.

In 2014, the league—whose official Twitter account has nearly 27 million followers—started putting its @NBA handle on the official game balls. The NBA also became the first organization—sports or otherwise—to boast one billion Vine views.

Vine and Amplify were just the beginning of Twitter's new focus on video. In 2015, Twitter bought another new video product that was about to launch: Periscope. An app that enables users to post streaming video from their phones, Periscope was an instant success. Within four months of launching, more than 10 million Periscope accounts had been created. The company announced that the amount of time users spent watching videos on Periscope amounted to 40 years per day!

While Periscope gave users the ability to post videos, Twitter's next big video splash was live streaming major events—in sports, news, and entertainment. In 2016, the NFL became Twitter's first live streaming partner when a deal was made to stream the league's Thursday Night Football games on Twitter. The NFL went in a different direction in 2017, selling the Thursday Night package to Amazon, but they continued to work with Twitter to create live and on-demand video exclusively for Twitter.

Twitter has continued to expand its video offerings. They streamed the 2016 US presidential debates. Through a deal with Live Nation, they offered streaming live concerts. During the solar eclipse in August 2017, they partnered with the Weather Channel to livestream the eclipse as it moved across the United States.

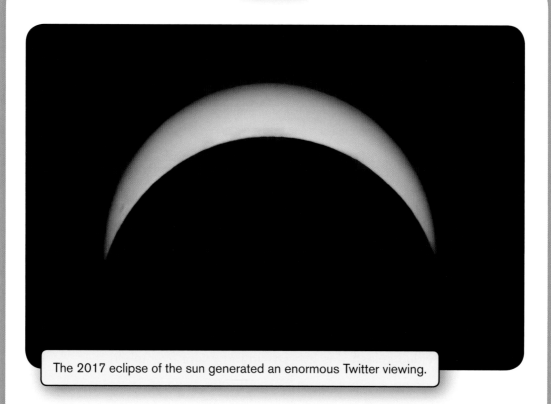

The 2017 eclipse of the sun generated an enormous Twitter viewing.

The increased use of video on Twitter helped transition the platform from a "second-screen experience" to a "first-screen experience." The company still encourages TV viewers to tweet while watching their favorite TV shows. But now users could tweet about events and programs they were watching directly on Twitter. Through a new offering called "Moments," tweets could be filtered into a live stream. From a sports standpoint, it's almost like being in a virtual sports bar.

In July 2017, Twitter announced that it had aired 1,200

hours of live video from April through June—twice as many as the previous three-month span, and they had 55 million unique viewers. Twitter co-founder Jack Dorsey was very excited about how users were engaging with video.

"We've gone head to head with a number of our competitors with the same exact content streaming at the same exact time, and we've been able to beat our competitors whether it's in sports, whether it's in news and politics, whether it's in esports because we have a different audience that's highly engaged with this content already and has an interest in it," Dorsey said.

Text-Dependent Questions

1. What was a key technical problem that Twitter had to solve early on; that is, what did they have to work hard to prevent from happening?

2. What is a retweet?

3. Name a major sports league that has partnered with Twitter.

Research Project

Sports leagues were early to the Twitter party. Visit Twitter or go online and research who else has teamed up. Find or identify five companies or services that use Twitter daily that are of interest to you and see what they are saying on their feeds.

4

The Consciousness of the World

Since so many people around the world use Twitter, the service truly is a reflection of life on Earth. There's good and bad and everything in between. The executives who run Twitter have always been guided by the philosophy that it's an open forum for people to express themselves, and therefore they mostly take a hands-off approach.

That said, media networks—even social media networks—have a responsibility to prevent their service from being used to spread harmful messages. Twitter has often had to address this issue, whether it be cyber-bullying, sexual harassment, or even terrorism.

"Abuse has no part on the service," Jack Dorsey said during a 2015 interview. "We have a staff of many that are dedicated to making sure that people feel safe and they can continue to trust the brand and the service to make sure their voices are heard everywhere in a way they want it to be heard, and they don't feel threatened in any way."

Over the years, Twitter has made improvements to functionality so that users can report abusers. Users have the ability to block certain accounts, so they don't have to see them. In extreme cases, Twitter has deleted accounts entirely.

"What we have to make sure of," Dorsey said, "is that everyone who participates in lending their voice to Twitter and using Twitter to amplify that

WORDS TO UNDERSTAND

prolific creating large numbers or quantities of something

voice, they feel safe doing so."

Dorsey recognizes the importance of Twitter "policing" its service, but he has always been wary of people thinking Twitter is the over-controlling bully. Even when it comes to terrorist groups using Twitter to promote extreme views, Dorsey believes it's something users can simply ignore.

"People should have the freedom to choose what they see and what they choose not to," he said. "It should not be forced upon them. . . . The more we start adding bias or editorial to the

President Trump has put Twitter in the headlines almost constantly.

service, the less people all over the world trust it. Trust is something we've really worked hard to earn and we will continue to do more of that and be very transparent around those policies."

Twitter's quest to promote free speech but also protect its users has been ongoing. The company has a safety division, and also formed the Trust and Safety Council, a group of outside organizations that advises Twitter on its policies against abuse.

Trump's Tweets

Of course, when it comes to free speech on Twitter, for better or worse, few users have been scrutinized quite like President Donald Trump. Even before the 2016 presidential election, Trump was known to be a **prolific** tweeter who never shied away from using the service to say what was on his mind. What has shocked people is that Trump maintained that style of tweeting after taking office. Some might say he actually took it to another level.

NBC News reported that in his first 100 days as president, there were only two days during which Trump did not send a tweet. In those 100 days, Trump tweeted more than 500 times from his account, @RealDonaldTrump.

In June 2017, Trump's personal Twitter attacks against a pair of MSNBC commentators led Democrats and Republicans alike to question his use of social media—calling his tweets "unpresidential." On July 1, Trump fired back with a series of Tweets:

Tech

2.0

"The FAKE & FRAUDULENT NEWS MEDIA is working hard to convince Republicans and others I should not use social media - but remember, I won....

....the 2016 election with interviews, speeches and social media. I had to beat #FakeNews, and did. We will continue to WIN! My use of social media is not Presidential - it's MODERN DAY PRESIDENTIAL. Make America Great Again!"

While Trump's tweets have often been personal attacks on members of the media or rival politicians, many of his tweets do address current events in America and around the world. News organizations follow @RealDonaldTrump closely and often have had to react to the tweets as part of their news coverage. At one point, former White House Press Secretary Sean Spicer declared that all of Trump's tweets should be considered "official statements by the president of the United States."

Trump has more than 41 million followers on Twitter, so it can be an effective means of communicating with the American public. In spite of having so many followers, Trump's preferred method of communicating with Americans has not been overwhelmingly popular. In July 2017, an ABC News/Washington Post poll revealed that 67 percent of Americans disapproved of the way Trump uses Twitter. In the same poll, 68 percent of respondents said his tweets were "inappropriate," 65 percent called them "insulting" and 52 percent said they were "dangerous."

Many people thought Trump crossed a line on September 23, 2017, using Twitter to possibly threaten North Korea when that country was coming under criticism for nuclear testing. Trump wrote in a tweet that if North Korea continued its nuclear testing, the country "wouldn't be around much longer." North Korean officials said Trump's tweet was the equivalent of a declaration of war.

That would certainly seem to qualify as a threatening tweet—and many people at the time urged Twitter to ban Trump's account. On September 25, Twitter's Public Policy account

Did Trump's tweets make it harder to relate to North Korea?

explained in a series of tweets that the "newsworthiness" of Trump's tweets made them acceptable:

"We hold all accounts to the same Rules, and consider a number of factors when assessing whether Tweets violate our Rules . . . Among the considerations is 'newsworthiness' and whether a Tweet is of public interest . . . This has long been internal policy and we'll soon update our public-facing rules to reflect it. We need to do better on this, and will . . . Twitter is committed to transparency and keeping people informed about what's happening in the world . . . We'll continue to be guided by these fundamental principles."

News brief on presidential tweeting

Happening Now

Whether it's the president's comments, live sporting events, breaking news, or just an anonymous user tweeting about what they're eating for lunch, Twitter has established itself as a global force. What has made Twitter a go-to social media network for hundreds of millions of people is the focus on things that are happening now.

So it makes perfect sense that one of Twitter's features is called Happening Now.

Twitter has always made it easy for users to follow current events, through Trending Topics, hashtag searches, and the Moments feature. Happening

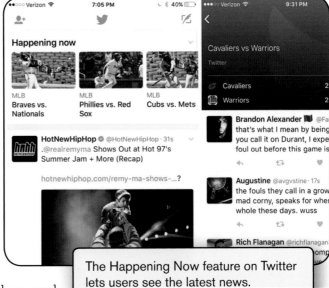

The Happening Now feature on Twitter lets users see the latest news.

Now advanced this concept and put the link at the top of users' timelines. Happening Now is based on an algorithm that reveals what people are talking about on Twitter. In other words, it's not Twitter steering the conversation but rather Twitter providing a window on the world.

"What's important to me about Twitter is that I think it's the closest thing that we have right now to a global consciousness, where you can actually see the world in real time," said Dorsey. "Not only can you see what's happening from a news level or from an event level, but you can actually see how people think and feel about it. And ultimately if we have more of that activity—and the nice thing about Twitter is you can share as much as you want—if we have more of that activity we can see how people live, what they desire and how they want to see the world, how they want to change the world, how they want to live in the world."

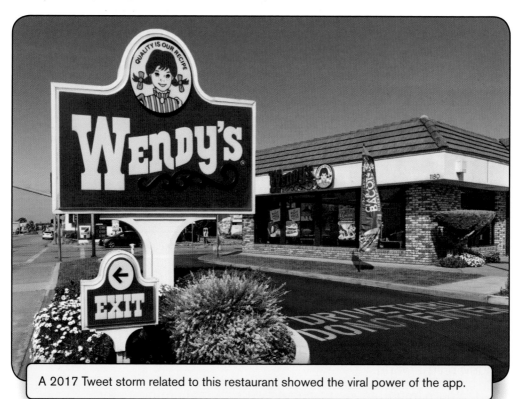

A 2017 Tweet storm related to this restaurant showed the viral power of the app.

Twitter with a Side of Chicken Nuggets

Strange as it may sound, Carter Wilkerson's quest for chicken nuggets may be the ultimate example of Twitter's impact on the world. His story includes so many aspects of what the medium is all about: communication, brand marketing, social good. How did a 16-year-old high school kid from Nevada set this in motion? Follow along:

On April 5, 2017, Wilkerson's craving for chicken nuggets led him to send a tweet directed at the fast-food chain Wendy's:

"How many retweets for a year of free chicken nuggets?"

To his surprise, @Wendys replied:

"18 million"

"I just thought of it as a silly joke to laugh at with my friends, so I replied, 'Consider it done,'" Wilkerson explained on his website. The rest, as they say, is history.

Wilkerson created the hashtag #NuggsforCarter, and it went viral. Not only were Wilkerson's friends retweeting it, so were celebrities and even big companies like Amazon and Microsoft. United Airlines retweeted it with an offer for Wilkerson that got some attention. They told him if he got the 18 million retweets they would fly him to any city in the world that had a Wendy's. Of course, 18 million retweets was unrealistic. The record to that point for most retweets—a selfie taken by Ellen DeGeneres posing with celebrities at the 2014 Academy Awards—was just over three million. On May 9, Twitter made it official, posting a blog that said Wilkerson's tweet set a new world record with 3.42 million retweets.

Considering all the free publicity Wendy's got from the #NuggsforCarter campaign, they went ahead and gave Wilkerson a gift card for a year's worth of free chicken nuggets. More notably, they made a $100,000 donation in Wilkerson's name to their official charity, the Dave Thomas Foundation for Adoption. For his part, Wilkerson has continued to raise money for charity, and the Twitter experience has given him that platform. Before

Taken at the 2016 Oscars, this group selfie rocketed around the world via Twitter.

his initial tweet to Wendy's, Wilkerson had 138 followers. Since then, he has more than 100,000 followers.

So an innocent tweet asking for free chicken nuggets got Wendy's a ton of free publicity, helped raise thousands of dollars for charity, and turned a high school kid into a social media celebrity. It would not have happened without Jack Dorsey's idea from a police scanner. What a long strange trip it has been, and one that is still continuing, 140 (or 280) characters at a time.

Text-Dependent Questions

1. What country did President Trump "threaten" via Twitter?

2. What is Twitter's Happening Now feature?

3. What fast-food restaurant was part of the experience described in the text?

Research Project

Time to make some poetry! Wander through Twitter feeds and pull out some of the most interesting or curious tweets. See if you put a string of them together to form a poem or a short story. Be creative! There are no wrong answers!

FIND OUT MORE

Books:

Bilton, Nick. *Hatching Twitter: A True Story of Money, Friendship, Power, and Betrayal.* New York: Portfolio, 2014.

Diaz-Ortiz, Claire. *Twitter for Good: Change the World One Tweet at a Time.* San Francisco: Jossey-Bass, 2011.

Tufecki, Zeynep. *Twitter and Tear Gas: The Power and Fragility of Networked Protest.* New Haven: Yale University Press, 2017.

On the Internet:

Twitter

http://www.twitter.com

"The End of Twitter"

https://www.newyorker.com/tech/elements/the-end-of-twitter

Jack Dorsey Interview with Bloomberg Businessweek

https://www.bloomberg.com/features/2016-jack-dorsey-twitter-interview/

SERIES GLOSSARY OF KEY TERMS

algorithm a process designed for a computer to follow to accomplish a certain task

colleagues the people you work with

entrepreneurs people who start their own businesses, often taking financial risks to do so

incorporate sold shares of stock to become a publicly traded company

innovation creativity; the process of building something new

open-source describing a computer program that can be used by any programmer to create or modify the product

perks benefits to doing something

startups new companies just starting out

targeting trying to reach a certain person or thing

venture capitalists people who invest money in young companies in hopes they will grow greatly in value

Tech 2.0

INDEX

140 characters, 8, 21, 26, 40-42, 61

Academy Awards, 46, 59

advertising, 34-35, 45

Amazon, 25, 59

Amplify, 45-47

celebrities, 29-31, 43, 59

citizen journalists, 27

CNN, 27, 29-30

Costolo, Dick, 33-34

Creamer, T.J., 28

cyber-bullying, 51-54

Dalai Lama, 30

Direct Messages, 39

Dorsey, Jack, 11-17, 22-23, 25, 32, 36, 38, 41, 49, 51-52, 58

Flight 1549, 27

followers, 22, 31

Game of Thrones, 44

Glass, Noah, 14

Happening Now, 57

Hashtags, 19, 38-39, 57

HBO, 44

Iran, 20-21

Jackson, Michael, 37

Kutcher, Ashton, 29-30

Lists, 42

longer tweets, 40-41

McCain, John, 17

Mendes, Shawn, 43

micro-blogging, 16, 21

Microsoft, 33, 59

Moments, 48, 57

MSNBC, 53

NASA, 28

NBA, 46-47

North Korea, 55

Obama, Barack, 17, 31

Obvious Corporation, 15

Odeo, 14, 25, 36

Periscope, 47

Perry, Katy, 31

Presidential debates, 47

programmers, 14, 36

Retweets, 39

SMS, 8, 14, 40

South by Southwest, 17, 25

Spicer, Sean, 54

Stone, Biz, 14-15, 29

Sullenberger, Chesley (Sully), 27

Super Bowl, 46

terrorism, 51-52

Trending Topics, 42, 57

Trump, Donald, 53-56

Trust and Safety Council, 53

TV networks, 27, 44, 46-47

Twitter, 7-9

    business of, 25, 31-35

    development of, 14-15

    features of, 39, 42

    growth of, 16-17, 37-38

    origins of, 11

    safety of, 51-53

    uses of, 18-22

URL shorteners, 42

venture capitalists, 25, 32

Vine, 43-44, 47

Wilkerson, Carter, 59-61

Williams, Evan, 15-16, 26, 32-33

Winfrey, Oprah, 29-30

Photo Credits

AP Photo: Steven Day 26. Dreamstime.com: Paulus Rusyanto 6; Pressureua 8; DrSerg 15; Cosmin Iftode 18; Sian Cox 19; Rrodrickbeiler 21; FeatureFlash 29; Joachim Eckel 30; Kianlin 36; Voyager624 38; Emevil 43; David Park 44; Alan Kolnik 48; Dave Bredeson 50; Kaspars Grinvalds 52; Christian Ouellet 55; Ken Wolter 58. NASA: 28. Newscom: Dennis Van Tine/LFI/Photoshoot 10; Rolf Vennenbernd/DPA/Picture-Alliance 22; Christian Charisius/DPA/Picture-Alliance 32; Ron Sachs/CNP/AdMedia 46; Instagram/UPI 60. Shutterstock: Guy J. Sagi 12; Alfie Photography 16; Gustavo Frazao 24.

About the Author

Craig Ellenport is a veteran journalist with 20 years' experience writing for the web. He has created and managed social media accounts for the National Football League, USA Basketball, and other media outlets.